Praise & Worship
HYMN SOLOS

15 Hymns Arranged for Solo Performance
by Stan Pethel

HOW TO USE THE CD ACCOMPANIMENT:

*A melody cue appears on the right channel only. If your CD player has a balance adjustment,
you can adjust the volume of the melody by turning down the right channel.*

ISBN 978-0-7935-9730-7

7777 W. BLUEMOUND RD. P.O. BOX 13819 MILWAUKEE, WI 53213

Visit Hal Leonard on the internet at http://www.halleonard.com

Praise & Worship
HYMN SOLOS

15 Hymns Arranged for Solo Performance
by Stan Pethel

CONTENTS

BLESSED BE THE NAME

Traditional

O FOR A THOUSAND TONGUES TO SING
Text by CHARLES WESLEY
Music by CARL G. GLASER

BRETHREN, WE HAVE MET TO WORSHIP

Words and Music by
WILLIAM MOORE

COME CHRISTIANS JOIN TO SING

Words by CHRISTIAN HENRY BATEMAN
Traditional Melody

COME, THOU FOUNT OF EVERY BLESSING

Words by ROBERT ROBINSON
Traditional Music compiled by JOHN WYETH

FAIREST LORD JESUS

Words for stanza 4 by JOSEPH AUGUST SEISS
Silesian Folk Melody
Arranged by RICHARD STORRS WILLIS

HOLY, HOLY, HOLY

Text by REGINALD HEBER
Music by JOHN B. DYKES

I NEED THEE EVERY HOUR

Words by ANNIE S. HAWKS
Music by ROBERT LOWRY

I STAND AMAZED IN THE PRESENCE

Words and Music by
CHARLES H. GABRIEL

MY FAITH LOOKS UP TO THEE

Words by RAY PALMER
Music by LOWELL MASON

O WORSHIP THE KING

Words by ROBERT GRANT
Based on Lyons,
Attributed to JOHANN MICHAEL HAYDN

PRAISE TO THE LORD, THE ALMIGHTY

Words by JOACHIM NEANDER
Music from Erneuerten Gesangbuch
Harmony by WILLIAM STERNDALE BENNETT

REJOICE YE PURE IN HEART

Words by EDWARD HAYES PLUMPTRE
Music by ARTHUR HENRY MESSITER

'TIS SO SWEET TO TRUST IN JESUS

Words by LOUISE M. R. STEAD
Music by WILLIAM J. KIRKPATRICK

TO GOD BE THE GLORY

Words by FANNIE J. CROSBY
Music by WILLIAM H. DOANE

WE HAVE HEARD THE JOYFUL SOUND

Words by PRISCILLA J. OWENS
Music by WILLIAM J. KIRKPATRICK

PLAY MORE OF YOUR FAVORITE SONGS

WITH GREAT INSTRUMENTAL PLAY ALONG PACKS FROM HAL LEONARD

Ballads
Solo arrangements of 12 songs: Bridge Over Troubled Water • Bring Him Home • Candle in the Wind • Don't Cry for Me Argentina • I Don't Know How to Love Him • Imagine • Killing Me Softly with His Song • Nights in White Satin • Wonderful Tonight • more.

00841445	Flute	$10.95
00841446	Clarinet	$10.95
00841447	Alto Sax	$10.95
00841448	Tenor Sax	$10.95
00841449	Trumpet	$10.95
00841450	Trombone	$10.95
00841451	Violin	$10.95

Band Jam
12 band favorites complete with accompaniment CD, including: Born to Be Wild • Get Ready for This • I Got You (I Feel Good) • Rock & Roll – Part II (The Hey Song) • Twist and Shout • We Will Rock You • Wild Thing • Y.M.C.A • and more.

00841232	Flute	$10.95
00841233	Clarinet	$10.95
00841234	Alto Sax	$10.95
00841235	Trumpet	$10.95
00841236	Horn	$10.95
00841237	Trombone	$10.95
00841238	Violin	$10.95

Disney Movie Hits
Now solo instrumentalists can play along with a dozen favorite songs from Disney blockbusters, including: Beauty and the Beast • Circle of Life • Cruella De Vil • Go the Distance • God Help the Outcasts • Kiss the Girl • When She Loved Me • A Whole New World • and more.

00841420	Flute	$12.95
00841421	Clarinet	$12.95
00841422	Alto Sax	$12.95
00841423	Trumpet	$12.95
00841424	French Horn	$12.95
00841425	Trombone/Baritone	$12.95
00841686	Tenor Sax	$12.95
00841687	Oboe	$12.95
00841426	Violin	$12.95
00841427	Viola	$12.95
00841428	Cello	$12.95

Prices, contents, and availability subject to change without notice.
Disney characters and artwork © Disney Enterprises, Inc.

Disney Solos
An exciting collection of 12 solos with full-band accompaniment on CD. Songs include: Be Our Guest • Can You Feel the Love Tonight • Colors of the Wind • Reflection • Under the Sea • You've Got a Friend in Me • Zero to Hero • and more.

00841404	Flute	$12.95
00841405	Clarinet/Tenor Sax	$12.95
00841406	Alto Sax	$12.95
00841407	Horn	$12.95
00841408	Trombone	$12.95
00841409	Trumpet	$12.99
00841410	Violin	$12.95
00841411	Viola	$12.95
00841412	Cello	$12.95
00841506	Oboe	$12.95
00841553	Mallet Percussion	$12.95

Easy Disney Favorites
13 Disney favorites for solo instruments: Bibbidi-Bobbidi-Boo • It's a Small World • Let's Go Fly a Kite • Mickey Mouse March • A Spoonful of Sugar • Toyland March • Winnie the Pooh • The Work Song • Zip-A-Dee-Doo-Dah • and many more.

00841371	Flute	$12.95
00841477	Clarinet	$12.95
00841478	Alto Sax	$12.95
00841479	Trumpet	$12.95
00841480	Trombone	$12.95
00841372	Violin	$12.95
00841481	Viola	$12.95
00841482	Cello/Bass	$12.95

Favorite Movie Themes
13 themes, including: *An American Symphony* from Mr. Holland's Opus • Braveheart • Chariots of Fire • Forrest Gump – Main Title • Theme from *Jurassic Park* • Mission: Impossible Theme • and more.

00841166	Flute	$10.95
00841167	Clarinet	$10.95
00841168	Trumpet/Tenor Sax	$10.95
00841169	Alto Sax	$10.95
00841170	Trombone	$10.95
00841171	F Horn	$10.95
00841296	Violin	$10.95

Jazz & Blues
14 songs: Cry Me a River • Fever • Fly Me to the Moon • God Bless' the Child • Harlem Nocturne • Moonglow • A Night in Tunisia • One Note Samba • Satin Doll • Take the "A" Train • Yardbird Suite • and more.

00841438	Flute	$12.95
00841439	Clarinet	$12.95
00841440	Alto Sax	$12.95
00841441	Trumpet	$12.95
00841442	Tenor Sax	$12.95
00841443	Trombone	$12.95
00841444	Violin	$12.95

Lennon and McCartney Solos
11 favorites: All My Loving • Can't Buy Me Love • Eleanor Rigby • The Long and Winding Road • Ticket to Ride • Yesterday • and more.

00841542	Flute	$12.99
00841543	Clarinet	$12.99
00841544	Alto Sax	$12.99
00841545	Tenor Sax	$12.99
00841546	Trumpet	$12.99
00841547	Horn	$12.99
00841548	Trombone	$12.99
00841549	Violin	$12.99
00841625	Viola	$12.99
00841626	Cello	$12.99

Movie & TV Themes
12 favorite themes: A Whole New World • Where Everybody Knows Your Name • Moon River • Theme from Schindler's List • Theme from Star Trek® • You Must Love Me • and more.

00841452	Flute	$10.95
00841454	Alto Sax	$10.95
00841455	Tenor Sax	$10.95
00841456	Trumpet	$10.95
00841458	Violin	$10.95

Sound of Music
9 songs: Climb Ev'ry Mountain • Do-Re-Mi • Edelweiss • The Lonely Goatherd • Maria • My Favorite Things • Sixteen Going on Seventeen • So Long, Farewell • The Sound of Music.

00841582	Flute	$11.95
00841583	Clarinet	$11.95
00841584	Alto Sax	$11.95
00841585	Tenor Sax	$11.95
00841586	Trumpet	$11.95
00841587	Horn	$11.95
00841588	Trombone	$11.95
00841589	Violin	$11.95
00841590	Viola	$11.95
00841591	Cello	$11.95

Worship Solos
11 top worship songs: Come, Now Is the Time to Worship • Draw Me Close • Firm Foundation • I Could Sing of Your Love Forever • Open the Eyes of My Heart • Shout to the North • and more.

00841836	Flute	$12.95
00841838	Clarinet	$12.95
00841839	Alto Sax	$12.95
00841840	Tenor Sax	$12.95
00841841	Trumpet	$12.95
00841843	Trombone	$12.95
00841844	Violin	$12.95
00841845	Viola	$12.95
00841846	Cello	$12.95

MORE FAVORITES FROM ESSENTIAL ELEMENTS

These superb collections feature favorite songs that students can play as they progress through their string method books. Each song is arranged to be played by either an orchestra or by soloists, with optional accompaniment on CD.

Each song appears twice in the book, featuring:
- Solo instrument version
- String arrangement for orchestra or ensembles
- Accompaniment CD included with conductor's score
- Accompaniment CD available separately
- Piano accompaniment book that is compatible with recorded backgrounds

Available:
- Conductor
- Violin
- Viola
- Cello
- String Bass

- Accompaniment CDs
- Value Starter Pak
  (includes 24 Student books plus Conductor Book w/CD

CHRISTMAS FAVORITES
Arranged by Lloyd Conley
Songs include:
The Christmas Song
  (Chestnuts Roasting
  on an Open Fire)
Frosty the Snow Man
A Holly Jolly Christmas
Jingle-Bell Rock
Let It Snow! Let It Snow! Let It Snow!
Rockin' Around the Christmas Tree
We Wish You a Merry Christmas

BROADWAY FAVORITES
Arranged by Lloyd Conley
Songs include:
Beauty and the Beast
Cabaret
Edelweiss
Get Me to the Church on Time
I Dreamed a Dream
Go Go Go Joseph
Memory
The Phantom of the Opera
Seventy Six Trombones

MOVIE FAVORITES
Arranged by Elliot Del Borgo
Includes themes from:
An American Tail
Chariots of Fire
Apollo 13
E.T.
Forrest Gump
Dances with Wolves
Jurassic Park
The Man from Snowy River
Star Trek
Mission: Impossible

PATRIOTIC FAVORITES
Arranged by John Moss
Songs include:
America, the Beautiful
Battle Hymn of the Republic
God Bless America
Hymn to the Fallen
My Country, 'Tis of Thee (America)
The Patriot
The Star Spangled Banner
Stars and Stripes Forever
This Is My Country
Yankee Doodle

FOR MORE INFORMATION, SEE YOUR LOCAL MUSIC DEALER, OR WRITE TO:

HAL•LEONARD® CORPORATION
7777 W. BLUEMOUND RD. P.O. BOX 13819 MILWAUKEE, WI 53213

Visit Hal Leonard Online at **www.halleonard.com**

Prices, contents, and availability subject to change without notice.
Some products may not be available outside the U.S.A.

0210